About Charles River

Charles River Editors provides superior editing and original writing services across the digital publishing industry, with the expertise to create digital content for publishers across a vast range of subject matter. In addition to providing original digital content for third party publishers, we also republish civilization's greatest literary works, bringing them to new generations of readers via ebooks.

Sign up here to receive updates about free books as we publish them, and visit Our Kindle Author Page to browse today's free promotions and our most recently published Kindle titles.

Introduction

Jumbo the Elephant

"I had often looked wistfully on Jumbo, but with no hope of ever getting possession of him, as I knew him to be a great favorite of Queen Victoria, whose children and grandchildren are among the tens of thousands of British juveniles whom Jumbo had carried on his back. I did not suppose he would ever be sold." – P.T. Barnum

Modern views of animals range from hunters who pay big money to go on safaris in Africa to vegans who refuse to use even the wool or milk from a fellow creature, and as is the case with most controversies, most people fall in the middle, not wanting to kick a dog but still enjoying a good steak. However, in the early 20th century, the standards were much different, with animals seen as strictly property to be gathered and used with little to no consideration about their health or feelings.

It was into this world that a little elephant later called Jumbo was born. He quickly learned the harsh realities of life when his mother was killed by hunters before his first birthday. Then he himself was taken from his sunny home and transported thousands of miles to soggy London, where he was expected to spend his days on display or earning his very limited keep by carrying small children for rides on his back. While he was fed hay, dry grass that was at least some substitute for the fresh greenery of the African plains, he was also fed both beer and hard liquor, oysters, cakes and candy, a diet that would have severely shortened his life had not a terrible accident ended it first.

During this time his one faithful friend, a man named Scott, tried to do the best he could to care for the animal and even meet his emotional needs. However, even Scott was hampered by the times in which he lived, especially when the command came to walk an 11 foot tall Jumbo into a crate barely big enough to hold him and to travel with him in these cramped quarters for a two week trip across another ocean to yet another unfamiliar land.

Ironically, it was that same trip that made Jumbo an international celebrity. Americans had loved traveling circuses for generations, and none represent the country's love for entertainment quite like the most famous of them all: the Ringling Bros. and Barnum & Bailey Circus. Circus promoters have long been viewed as somewhat shady hucksters, but none could top P.T. Barnum, who used a blend of traditional circus entertainment, freak show exhibits, and outright hoaxes to create "The Greatest Show on Earth". In fact, Barnum had specialized in circus entertainment decades before traveling circuses were truly a national sensation, particularly thanks to the popularity of the Barnum American Museum in New York City. Barnum's museum offered something for everyone across its different halls, from poetic readings to animal exhibits, and all the while, Barnum was defiant when confronted by criticism, reminding people, "I am a showman by profession...and all the gilding shall make nothing else of me."

Barnum introduced America to Jumbo, and the elephant subsequently became one of the most legendary acts in the history of the circus, as well as "exhibits" like Joice Heth, an elderly African American woman Barnum advertised as a 161 year old who nursed George Washington.

He also notoriously perpetrated hoaxes with General Tom Thumb and claimed to have a live mermaid, so it's no surprise that Barnum is often apocryphally quoted as saying, "There's a sucker born every minute." While he didn't actually say that, he said something similar: "Nobody ever lost a dollar by underestimating the taste of the American public."

Jumbo was not a pet to P.T. Barnum but an investment, an attraction that soon paid off in a big way. But Jumbo was also beginning to suffer the effects of his poor lifestyle even as fate led him toward his death on a crowded railroad track. It's a story that saddens many today, but in the 1880s, it was more or less the way things were. Nonetheless, the influence Jumbo had was fitting given his size, leading not only to similar acts across various traveling circuses but also to adaptations of his story, perhaps most notably Disney's *Dumbo* in the 1940s.

Jumbo the Elephant: The Life and Legacy of History's Most Famous Circus Animal looks at Jumbo's history, and the giant impact the elephant had on entertainment. Along with pictures of important people, places, and events, you will learn about Jumbo like never before, in no time at all.

Jumbo the Elephant: The Life and Legacy of History's Most Famous Circus Animal

About Charles River Editors

Introduction

   Chapter 1: The Most Famous Pachyderm Ever

   Chapter 2: A World Famous Attraction

   Chapter 3: The Jumbo Craze

   Chapter 4: Bon Voyage

   Chapter 5: The Largest Living Mountain of Flesh to Travel the United States

   Chapter 6: I Had My Doubts

   Online Resources

   Bibliography

Chapter 1: The Most Famous Pachyderm Ever

"Probably the most famous pachyderm ever kept in captivity was the six-and-a-half-ton African elephant, Jumbo, which had come to the London Zoo as a baby, standing only about four feet high and weighing less than 700 pounds. At first he was rather troublesome but after a short time became perfectly manageable and grew very rapidly. Mr. Bartlett, the director of the garden, attributed this to good food and a daily bath in hot weather. In sixteen years he grew from four to eleven feet in height. Then the London Zoo sold him to an American circus, despite the fact that he had become their prime attraction. The reason lay in the fact that Jumbo was given to fits of excitement and terrified everybody who came near him except his keeper, Mathew Scott, who had extraordinary control over him. It was feared that if Scott fell ill, or was injured by the animal, the creature would be entirely unmanageable, for no other man dared go near him in his house. At night he would tear about and almost shake the house down. After becoming the property of Mr. Barnum, however, Jumbo's temperament seemed to change, probably due to the harder work and exercise which went with the life of a traveling circus. He became quite tractable and was exhibited all over Europe and America." - William M. Mann, *Wild Animals in and out of the Zoo* (1930)

Most biographies begin with the date and place of birth of the celebrity being described, but in the case of Jumbo the Elephant, this information is missing, for young Jumbo was born in secret, with only his pachyderm mother in attendance, somewhere in East Africa, likely near the Setit River. Prevailing wisdom speculates that he entered the world sometime around Christmas in 1860, but while he was still young, he lost his mother to hunters who chose to spare his life, likely in the hopes of hunting him down when he was full grown.

However, in a stroke of fate that changed his future, the infant elephant was captured by Taher Sheiff, a Sudanese hunter who was contracted to sell the infant to a zoo. Sheriff found a buyer in Samuel White Baker, a British explorer who in February 1862 purchased the young elephant. Baker later wrote, "I was much interested with the tame elephants, which are taught to assist in various works, and are employed for moving huge stones into position, when building bridges, in road-making through the interior." When Baker bought the young elephant, he noted that he was about four feet tall and estimated his weight as 500 pounds. If his figures are accurate, and young Jumbo was developing normally, the little bull elephant would have been about a year old.

Ondřej Žváček's picture of the Setit River on the border of Ethiopia and Eritrea

Baker

One of the things that made Jumbo stand out during his month in the camp was how well adjusted he was. Having lived most of his life in the presence of humans, he was neither fearful nor aggressive around them. When the time came for the caravan to move on, the young elephant was allowed to walk alongside without any sort of rope holding him, with his captor unafraid that he would escape.

The group of men and beasts made it 300 miles across the desert to the port of Suakin, on the Red Sea, where an animal dealer named Lorenzo Casanova took possession of him and placed him on a ship bound for the Suez, 500 miles away.

A depiction of Suakin as it appeared in 1884

The conditions in the ship's hold, where the animals were kept, were miserable, to the point that it's somewhat surprising any of them survived. At Alexandria, the little elephant sailed with his surviving cohorts to Trieste, Austria, where they were loaded on a train and shipped to Dresden. There, Prussian dealer Gottlieb Kreutzberg bought the entire lot, soon selling Jumbo to the Jardin des Plantes in Paris sometime in the fall of 1862. He arrived at the zoo a few months later, only to disappoint his new owners, who had assumed an elephant of any age would be huge. His future owner, P. T. Barnum later wrote, "He was consigned to the Jardin des Plantes, in Paris, and when he arrived there he was a funny little animal that attracted no particular notice." Still, he was placed in the Rotunda for Large Herbivores along with a number of other large animals from Africa and the Middle East.

Kreutzberg

By the time Jumbo arrived in Paris, the young elephant had received his name, Jumbo, perhaps while he was still in Africa, perhaps later. No one really knows how he came to be called that, although it could be a variation for the Swahilli word for chief, "jumbe."

Vincent Zimmermann's picture of Jumbo's Paris home.

Jumbo remained in Paris until April 1865, when inspectors declared his surroundings unfit and insisted that at least some of the now five elephants kept in the rotunda be sent to other museums. This information reached the head of the London Zoological Gardens at Regent's Park. He had long wanted an African elephant and agreed to exchange some of his animals for the still young elephant. Matthew Scott, who was sent by the London Zoo to receive Jumbo, wrote of that first meeting, "When I first saw Jumbo I met him on the coast of France. He was about being brought from that country to England for medical care — to your humble servant, the animals' physician. A more deplorable, diseased, and rotten creature never walked God's earth, to my knowledge. Jumbo had been presented to France, together with another baby elephant, when they were quite infants. When he was given in my charge, outside of Paris, his condition was simply filthy. He had been in the care of Frenchmen for several years, and they either did not know how to treat the race of elephants, or culpably neglected his raising. I don't know which, but when I met him in France I thought I never saw a creature so woe-begone, The poor thing was full of disease, which had worked its way through the animal's hide, and had almost eaten out its eyes. The hoofs of the feet and the tail were literally rotten, and the whole hide was so covered with sores…"

In his record of his relationship for Jumbo, Scott tended toward the flowery language popular at that time. "I received him kindly, took him tenderly over the Channel, and lodged him in a comfortable, clean bed in my stable. I undertook to be his doctor, his nurse, and general servant. I watched and nursed him night and day with all the care and affection of a mother (if it were possible for a man to do such a thing), until by physicking from the inward centre of his frame I cleared out all diseased matter from his lungs, liver, and heart. I then, by means of lotions of oil, etc., took all the scabs from the roots of his almost blinded eyes. I removed his leprous coat as cleanly as a man takes off an overcoat; and his skin was as fine as that of a horse just from the clipper's, after the hair had been cut off. I was rewarded by having a clean-shaven looking creature in a perfectly sound state of mind and body ; and he required no blanket nor overcoat, although he was far, far from home, in a much more northerly climate than his native element in ' Afric's Sunny Sands.' Taking climate and covering into account, it was like transferring a man from the western shores of the Atlantic to 'Greenland's Icy Mountains.'"

Scott and Jumbo soon became lifelong friends, as noted by Barnum: "After he had been for a few months at the Zoological Garden, he and his keeper, Mr. Scott, were one day photographed, and in the picture it is shown that the keeper stood a breast higher than Jumbo. All at once, however, a sudden spurt of growing came over him, just as ordinary-sized boys in a family suddenly grow up into giants; and Jumbo grew, and grew, and grew, until he got to be twelve feet high, fourteen feet long, eighteen feet around the middle of his body, and reached the very respectable aldermanic-elephantine weight of seven tons."

Jumbo and Scott in 1865

Chapter 2: A World Famous Attraction

"Even before he was purchased by the American showman P. T. Barnum in 1892, Jumbo the elephant was a world-famous attraction at the London Zoo.... His name became part of our language, all but replacing 'mammoth' as a synonym for immense, thus contributing to the durable oxymoron 'jumbo shrimp.' ... Natural history was a popular craze. As the study of God's creations, it was considered morally uplifting and compatible with Victorian notions of respectability. Young and old, especially 'ladies,' collected shells and butterflies, pressed flowers, and raised hothouse orchids. Nature study was even healthful, prompting walks along the seashore or bird-watching tours through fields and woods. Victorian parlors displayed aquariums, fern collections, butterfly cases, albums of seaweed, and popular books on natural history. Zoological and botanical parks flourished as thousands flocked to marvel at rare and unfamiliar species brought from the corners of the Empire." - "Victorian England's Hippomania," *Natural History*, February 1993

Once in London, Jumbo became popular with children of all walks of life, from street urchins to royalty. The staid Queen Victoria even allowed her youngest children, Prince Leopold and Princess Beatrice, to visit the zoo and ride on Jumbo's giant saddle, called a howdah. The zoo knew that it had a good thing in the elephant, so it jumped at the chance to buy another one. This time it was a female, whom the owners named Alice after the title character of *Alice's Adventures in Wonderland*, then a bestseller. According to Scott, "Her name is Alice. She is a native of the west coast of Africa, and was born in the year of our Lord one thousand eight hundred and sixty -four, the same year that Jumbo — nearly four years old — was brought to me. She was born in the midst of a tribe of wild elephants that roamed about and sported in the freedom of their native element in the region spoken of above. ... The arrival of this female baby elephant — not a year old— caused me great joy, and I cannot find words to express to my readers the pleasure and happiness I experienced at beholding my Jumbo's delight when he first saw Alice coming along. ...when I passed by Jttmbo's stable, where he roamed at leisure, the moment lie saw Alice led along toward him, I thought he would have broken that stable front out to get at us. ... Jumbo and Alice lived very happily together in the Zoological Gardens, London, for about seventeen years...."

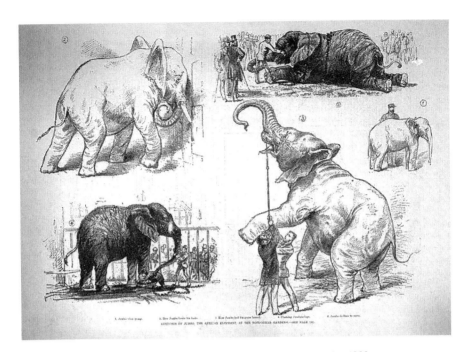

Sketches of Jumbo in the *London News*, February 25, 1882

As Jumbo grew, it became imperative that he be trained to both obey Scott and put on a show for the zoo's patrons. One of the most delightful events came in the summer, when Scott would take Jumbo out of the zoo and lead him down to the River Thames, where the giant pachyderm would amuse audiences by frolicking happily in the water. Scott observed, "Jumbo knows how to bathe and swim; I may say he is a 'great swimmer.' He makes a bigger hole in the water than most other animals, and he certainly throws water up into the air higher than any other animal, with his great waterspout trunk."

Unfortunately, the reality of Jumbo's life was not quite as rosy as the picture Scott paints. In fact, when he had been at the zoo for a year, some of the keepers there complained that the elephant was actually rather moody and would even fly into rages at times, especially when forced into his stable. He even tried to break out on a few occasions. Since he seemed happy in the water, the decision was made to make the most of that and, according to Scott, "it was arranged to construct a special bath for him and Alice, his wife."

Once in this new environment, the elephant seemed happier. Scott noted, "Jumbo would, every now and then, turn right about and with his massive trunk throw up such a quantity of water as would make a shower-bath fall on Alice's back, and then, perhaps, he would in the same way, throw up to a great height a regular three-inch water-pipe gush of a…bath, and this would so tickle Alice, and so add to her enjoyment, that she would presently begin to reciprocate; but as her trunk and powers were not so great as Jumbo's, she could not make such a good job of it. Yet Jumbo was awfully pleased at Alice's consideration in trying thus to wash his back. Jumbo would make a good five- or six-story window- washer. When they got to swimming depth they would play some of the funniest frolics, rolling about like two ships in a storm at sea; and at other times would swim most majestically along, Jumbo always leading the way. for quite a time, then, when they got to the end of the oblong bath, Alice would turn round and Jumbo would follow her back to walking depth ; then some more shower-bath business, and after that a return for a few dives."

Jumbo's training regimen was part of Scott's purview, and he was eventually able to work with the elephant enough that by the middle of 1866, the zoo felt it was safe to offer rides on the creature's back. Part of what made Jumbo appear so gentle was that he never grew long tusks, having broken one in an accident and then keeping both rubbed down short. Scott later assured his readers, "Jumbo has had no idle days for 'loafing' or hanging around stores or otherwise wasting his time. He has been engaged in carrying around the children of the human family almost daily for twenty years, and I suppose no animal has ever carried so many on his back as Jumbo. Certainly I can claim for him that no animal ever did his work more affectionately or tenderly, and freer from accident. … Jumbo is a very careful walker, and always looks where he is going, and, like some others of God's creatures, is rather slow in his movements, but both very sure footed and thoughtful. … Jumbo never gets excited when he is attending to children."

Indeed Jumbo did not "loaf," since Scott was allowed to keep all the money he charged for rides. At the same time, the human offered Jumbo the best of treatment for the time period, even coming to the zoo on his days off to make sure the elephant was being properly cared for.

The most important part of caring for Jumbo was, of course, feeding him. According to a later Barnum publication, by the early 1870s the still growing elephant was eating "200 pounds of hay, 1 barrel of potatoes, 2 bushels of oats, 15 loaves of bread, a slew of onions and several pails of water. He consumed a gallon or two of whiskey per day when Scott felt health concerns warranted it." These were the years of his most significant growth, and by 1882, the elephant was a full 12 feet tall and weighed 12,000 pounds.

As Jumbo grew, so did the problems he caused Bartlett at the London Zoo. The director had originally wanted to make the animal his own pet project, but Scott's attachment to Jumbo and vice versa made that impossible. By 1882, the elephant was the largest animal in captivity and a major sensation. At the same time, Bartlett knew that the animal was also nearing what might best be described as "elephant adolescence," known scientifically as musth. During this period, glandular changes often cause otherwise tame beasts to become increasingly violent, and there were already problems with his behavior anytime Scott was not around, leading the trainer to comment that "one of Jumbo's faults is that when I am out of his sight, or rather when I go away, he knows it, and if I don't come back at regular times he always makes me aware of it, both day and night. ...if I am an hour or two overdue after the time he is looking for me, he commences to whine and cry, and becomes very naughty...." Part of the issue might also have been that he molars were coming in in an unusual manner and were likely to have been painful.

With all these concerns on his mind, Bartlett decided to sell Jumbo if he could find a buyer. He would indeed find one, and it would set off controversies of all kinds.

Chapter 3: The Jumbo Craze

"Mr. Barnum explained that it was perhaps known to all of his hearers that the 'Jumbo craze' in England had no parallel in either ancient or modern history. Everybody in the British Isles talked or wrote of Jumbo, and his departure was looked upon us a public calamity. Women and children wept, and old men bowed their heads in grief. Royalty was shocked. Poets sang Jumbo's praises, and artists illustrated books filled with events in the life of the best-known elephant in the world. Everybody, from royalty to the lowest depths of London wore Jumbo scarf-pins and sleeve-buttons, and the people dreamed of him. To all this Mr. Scott and Mr. Newman nodded assent. Then they told of the bags of letters which they had received from weeping women and children who wrote to beg them, to carefully watch over 'poor Jumbo.' Mr. Scott showed a photograph of Jumbo and himself taken when the heart Was 4 years of age. Then Mr. Scott was taller than the elephant. The keeper's eyes were watery as he displayed the picture. He admitted, when Mr. Barnum spoke of It, that after Jumbo had been purchased by the American showman something like $50,000 was received at the Royal Zoological Gardens from those who desired to see Jumbo." - *New York Times*, April 9, 1882

Barnum

The London Zoo was popular with more than the locals, and one of the fans was the famous American showman P. T. Barnum, who already had decades of experience with circuses and similar forms of entertainment. Of course, to call Barnum merely a showman is selling him short, because during the course of his adventurous life, he was a shrewd businessman, a politician, and the country's most famous and notorious promoter of both entertainment and himself.

Ironically, Barnum was 61 years old by the time he found the calling that he's still most closely associated with. Barnum was visiting some friends in Delavan, Wisconsin when he met William Cameron Coup, and the two men hit it off so quickly that they decided to go into business together. Since Barnum was the famous one, they called their venture the "P. T. Barnum's Grand Traveling Museum, Menagerie, Caravan & Hippodrome", and it was just what it claimed to be: a strange mélange of circus, museum and freak show. As if its first name was not long and descriptive enough, it would later be known as "P.T. Barnum's Travelling World's Fair, Great Roman Hippodrome and Greatest Show On Earth."

Coup

An 1882 advertisement of Coup's circus.

Rather than build a permanent structure, Barnum would take the museum, complete with exotic animals and human oddities, on the road, and he added in a variety show with trapeze artists, jugglers, trained dogs, and bareback horse riders. In April 1871, P.T. Barnum's Grand Traveling Museum, Menagerie, Caravan, and Circus debuted in Brooklyn. The show was performed under canvas tents, filling three acres of land. Barnum's circus was the largest circus ever seen in the U.S.

When the circus hit the road, 100 wagons rolled across the East and the Midwest. At the end of its first year, the circus had grossed an astounding $400,000 in ticket sales. A year later, Barnum's circus took advantage of the railroad boom that the country saw in the years following the Civil War. Now, it took only a day to load up the five-acre show and speed it off to its next engagement. When the circus train arrived at its next destination, watching the parade of animals disembark from the cars and make their way to the location of the show was almost as exciting as the circus itself.

After a decade of traveling around on his own, in 1881, Barnum merged with James Anthony Bailey, who was the manager of the "Cooper and Bailey Circus". James Bailey had been around the circus his entire life after being orphaned as a young boy and taken in by the nephew of Hachaliah Bailey, who was considered a pioneer of the modern circus. In his 20s, Bailey started a business association with James Cooper, and the two of them opened the Cooper and Bailey Circus. Bailey was also an astute businessman who understood that by purchasing smaller shows that might take away from his own business, he could transform himself into an entertainment mogul.

Barnum watched this with a mixture of envy and admiration, because as successful as he was, Bailey was even more so, taking in twice the money that Barnum did. When Cooper and Bailey owned the Great London Circus, they upped the ante in their rivalry with Barnum by adding a baby elephant named Columbia to the show. Barnum could not top that, so he did the next best thing by trying to buy the elephant. By this time, Cooper was no longer in the picture, and Bailey was looking for someone else to team up with, so the two men formed a venture with an even longer name: "P.T. Barnum's Greatest Show On Earth, And The Great London Circus, Sanger's Royal British Menagerie and The Grand International Allied Shows United." Perhaps not surprisingly, this cumbersome name was ultimately shortened to simply "Barnum & Bailey's".

Bailey

In 1881, "The Greatest Show on Earth" debuted and performed from New York, into the Midwest, and as far south as Texas. This new circus was the largest of its kind, exhibiting constant action in three rings instead of the standard one or two, and in a *New York Herald* review, it was reported that the only negative aspect of the show was that there was almost too much to see, and watching one act meant missing out on another. It was also about to add the biggest act of them all.

Barnum recalled the process through which he bought Jumbo: "During my visits to London I had often seen the famous big elephant, and had ridden on him, but it never entered my head that I could buy him. I eventually told my agent to approach Mr. Bartlett. the Superintendent of the Gardens, on the subject. He conferred with the Council of the Gardens, and they accepted my offer of $10,000 for the animal. In view of the results of this enterprise, it seems a little singular, but the fact is, my partner, Mr. Hutchinson, was strongly opposed to buying Jumbo. 'What is the difference,' he would say, 'between an elephant seven feet high and another eleven or twelve feet high? — an elephant is an elephant.' I insisted that this was the greatest beast in the world, and urged that, being such, Barnum's Circus couldn't afford to be without him. Finally the objections of my partner were overruled and we sent over the money to pay for Jumbo."

Even after the deal was struck, it was hardly done, because when Londoners heard that a zoo favorite was being sold across the ocean, they were outraged. Children wrote letters to Queen Victoria asking her not to allow the sale, and musicians wrote songs like "Why Part with Jumbo?" The *London Evening News* complained on February 27, 1882, "We are seldom able to agree with Mr. Ruskin on any public question, and it is still rarer for Mr. Ruskin to agree with the public; but on the question of Jumbo he has given expression to what is doubtless the prevailing sentiment. No case was ever feebler than that for the expatriation of Jumbo. The arguments which have been brought forward to prove that he cannot be kept any longer in the Zoological Gardens are perfectly contemptible, and would not justify a procedure resolution. The position of those who have made this stupid bargain appears to be based on the following singular grounds: first, that Jumbo is approaching an age when elephants are apt to become dangerous; secondly, that Mr. Barnum has offered £2,000 for him, thirdly, that there are no conveniences at the Zoo for keeping dangerous elephants and no means for ensuring the safety of children who ride on Jumbo's back. The ethics of the argument are about on a par with the logic. Are Yankee children then of less account in the eye; of Yankee showmen than English children in the eyes of the Zoological Society? Are the resources of Barnum greater than those of British civilization? If Barnum can take care of Jumbo, why not Mr. Sclater? Elephants are surely no very strange animals, of unknown habits or unfamiliar to society. We keep hundreds of them in India, and find no difficulty in restraining them during the periods when they become wild."

The *Evening News*, always willing to take a political shot, continued, "That elephants are disposed to fits of 'must' is perfectly well known. Prime Ministers also have their fits of 'must' but no one suggests selling them to Barnum. We know by certain signs, in both cases, when the fit is coming on; and we know, or ought to know, how to treat it, at least in the case of the larger pachyderm. It is absurd that a Society like the Zoological cannot command the means of keeping one male elephant in safety during the temporary period when he suffers a constitutional derangement. It is simply a question of thickness of timber and strength of iron, as easy of solution in a country like England, by an association like the Zoological, with its large funds and all the accumulated experience of centuries at its disposal, as it can be in America by a travelling showman. We must protest that in this matter the Society and the experts are wholly wrong and the public sentiment is entirely right. Jumbo ought not to be allowed to go if he prefers to stay; and it becomes fairly a responsibility for the law whether the cruelty which has already been practiced on the poor brute should be permitted to be renewed. That Jumbo may continue to foil all the efforts made to shut him up, to torture him, to coerce him, let us fervently pray."

A few weeks later, on March 4, the *London North News and Finsbury Gazette* responded, "'Gush' on the text of the monstrous elephant Jumbo has tilled columns of the Daily Telegraph all week, procured the insertion of a letter or two in the Times, and extracted a warning note from the irrepressible Mr. Ruskin. Jumbo, we have it on the best authority, is the tallest elephant ever known in Europe and probably India. Those who know the character of the authorities at the Zoological Gardens, and particularly of the curator, the am able enthusiast, Mr. Bartlett, are quite sure that it is not Mr. Barnum's [money] that has tempted them to part with this enormous and popular beast. They know the character of the animal a great deal better than these gushers from Mr. Ruskin downwards to the writers in the Daily Telegraph, and are quite above all mercenary motives. The Zoo is a scientific, not a dividend-paying company. If Mr. Barnum's men do succeed in getting Jumbo away to America, his attractions have been famously advertised and tremendously increased."

Barnum himself weighed in on the controversy, sending a telegram to one newspaper, which it printed. His missive read, "My compliments to Editor Daily Telegraph and British Nation. Fifty millions of American citizens anxiously awaiting Jumbo's arrival. My forty years' invariable practice of exhibiting best that money could procure makes Jumbo's presence here imperative. Hundred thousand pounds would be no 'inducement to cancel purchase. My largest tent seats thirty thousand persons, and is filled twice each day. It contains four rings, in three of which three full circus companies give different performances simultaneously In the large outer ring or racing track the Roman Hippodrome is exhibited. In two other immense connecting tents my colossal zoological collection and museum are shown. In December next I visit Australia in person, with Jumbo and my entire mammoth combination of seven shows, via California, thence through Suez Canal. Following summer to London. I shall then exhibit in. every prominent city in Great Britain. May afterwards return Jumbo to his old position in Royal Zoological Gardens. Wishing long life and prosperity to the British Nation, the Daily Telegraph, and Jumbo, I am, the public's obedient servant, 'P. T. BARNUM.'"

Looking back on the events surrounding Jumbo's departure, Barnum himself later admitted, When the English people got information that Jumbo was to be taken out of the country, they were fairly wild with excitement. Many newspapers looked upon it as an outrage, and blamed the Superintendent of the Gardens, the Council, and everyone who had had anything to do with the affair. The great art critic John Ruskin took part in the discussion, and said that England was not accustomed to sell her pets. There was so much dissatisfaction expressed, that the Zoological Garden people tried to induce my agent to rescind the sale, but I told them I could not; I had announced the purchase of the elephant and I could not afford to disappoint the American people. The stockholders of the Zoological Garden held a meeting. They insisted that the Council had no right to sell without their consent, and got out an injunction on us, which, by some legal hocus-pocus which it would require too much space here to explain, came up in the Court of Chancery, which he stated that all the British children were distressed at the elephant's departure: on what terms would I return Jumbo? 'Answer, prepaid, unlimited.' When I read the last three words of this dispatch, I am afraid that the spirit of practical joking took possession of me for the moment. I took the Englishman at his word and answered unlimited.' I told him that a hundred thousand pounds would not induce me to cancel my purchase, and then I gave him a pretty full description of my circus, commencing, 'My largest tent seats 20,000 persons,' etc., etc., and ended with ' wishing long life and prosperity to the British nation, the Telegraph and Jumbo." This dispatch was published in the Telegraph the next morning, and it was republished on the following day in the principal newspapers throughout Great Britain."

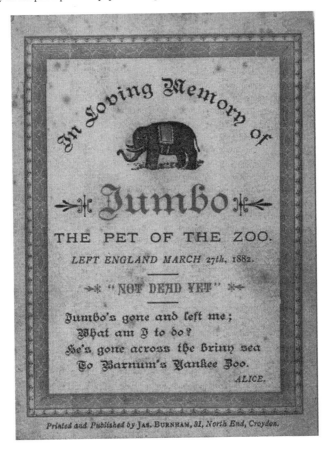

A Jumbo Trade Card "signed" by Alice

Jumbo in 1882

Chapter 4: Bon Voyage

"In the dawn of a fine spring morning we started on our journey to the New World. The box was drawn by sixteen horses, and the weight was as much as they could draw. Thousands followed Jumbo to the river-bank, expressing their regrets at his departure. The grief of the children was really sorrowful. At Gravesend Jumbo held a levee, and a very fashionable one too, for a distinguished company came on board the steamer to wish him bon voyage. ... Jumbo was somewhat alarmed at first by the noise of the machinery and the rolling of the steamship; but I was always at his side, and managed to calm him so that he became quite a sailor when he got his sea legs on. We arrived at last, and Jumbo seemed to be delighted. He trumpeted out his joy, as much as to say, 'Ah! Mr. Scott, we are at last in the ' land of the free and the home of the brave.' When Jumbo's house was hoisted on the dock ten horses were hitched to the car upon which it was placed. Then two of his brother elephants, called ' pushers,' put their immense heads to the back of the house, and at a signal the horses commenced to draw and the elephants to push ; and after an hour's work we arrived at Madison Square Garden, where Jumbo was released from his narrow quarters, and seemed so joyful at his freedom that he twined his trunk around me in an ecstasy of delight." - Scott

An illustration of Jumbo being transported to America

No matter what the British people thought of the situation, Jumbo was now Barnum's property, and he wasted no time in preparing to ship him to America, which ended up costing him another $20,000. The first step was to build a crate that could hold the giant beast; though modern sensibilities to animal comfort might be horrified by this prospect, this was standard procedure during the 19th century. The crate was only a little larger than Jumbo himself and allowed precious little opportunity for movement. Fortunately, it was not completely enclosed but instead was covered with iron bars at either end.

A newspaper illustrations of Jumbo in the crate

The next step was for Barnum to find a ship willing to carry his giant cargo. The *Times* later reported, "Passage for Jumbo was first engaged on the Persian Monarch. Then Jumbo declined to make the trip, and this aroused the affectionate interest of all England." This incident proved to be one of the most amusing and sad events surrounding his departure, for when the time came for Jumbo to leave his home in the Zoo on February 18, he simply refused to go. His keepers thought he might change his mind the next day, but he still would not budge. He took a few steps into one of the streets running through the zoo and then laid down, much to the delight of the crowd. Perhaps encouraged by the cheers and attention, Jumbo remained in his comfortable position for a full week.

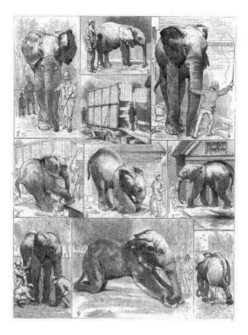

**"Jumbo's pitiful refusal to leave London Zoo tugged at the nation's heartstrings"
(Magazine illustration, 1882)**

Panicked, Bill Newman cabled Barnum for instructions and was told by the great showman, "Let him stay there as long as he wants. It's great publicity." Barnum himself later wrote, "It did its part in keeping up the excitement. Jumbo had never been out of the Garden since the day he had entered it, twenty years before. When my agents attempted to get him out he would not stir; he seemed to know instinctively that something extraordinary was going to happen. My agent cabled me: 'Jumbo is lying in the Garden and will not stir. What shall we do?' I replied: 'Let him lie there as long as he wants to.'.' All this, it will be observed, kept up public interest. Then we built a cage on wheels, and sank the wheels into the ground, leaving both ends of the cage open. It was many days before he could be induced to walk through. We let him get used to going through for several days and finally shut him in. It took a score of horses to pull the cage out of the earth, after we had dug around the wheels, and we dragged the cage down to the wharf. There

Jumbo met a whole crowd of his admirers, including such fashionable people as Lady Burdett-Coutts, who brought him cakes and dainties. One enthusiast testified his affection by sending some champagne and oysters. On the vessel we had to cut away a part of the deck above his lodgings to make his apartment large enough. The original price of Jumbo was $10,000; his final cost was $30,000. He paid for himself the first ten days after his arrival."

Still, Newman's patience eventually wore out, and he threatened to fire Scott if the elephant did not move. The following day, the faithful trainer persuaded his charge to walk into the confining crate. A London publication, *Lloyd's Weekly*, reported, "The task of placing Jumbo in the box prepared for transporting him to the docks was successfully accomplished on Wednesday morning. The structure measures 13 feet in length, six in breadth, and about 11 in height. Jumbo having been chained up by the fore-legs on the previous day, he could offer comparatively little resistance when he was hobbled. This preliminary operation, which was adroitly managed by "Elephant Bill," assisted by Scott and two other keepers, was rendered necessary, not only to close the mouth, but in order that the trunk, with which an infuriated elephant might inflict serious injuries, should not be allowed to have full play. On arriving fairly inside his structure, he was brought to a standstill in the centre, and in a surprisingly short space of time he was fastened to the iron-bound beams on each side by his forelegs with the hobbles by which he had been previously secured in his house. He was now effectually fixed inside his carriage, but much remained to be done before he was ready to be moved.

Scott and Jumbo standing around and in a crate outside the London Zoo

Jumbo's aggravations were far from an end, and those watching could only feel a mixture of sadness and respect for the way in which he resisted the indignities being thrust on him. The article noted, "The hind-legs, to begin with, had to be lassoed with a rope, in order that they might be held previously to being attached to the box by chains in the same manner as the forelegs. First one of his hind-legs was secured, and the second had been caught in a rope passed in and out of the iron railings and pulled by half a dozen of the men, when Jumbo, who had just then appeared to be getting tired of resistance, put forth all his strength in one mighty effort and fairly broke the rope, which snapped with a report like that of a pistol-shot. The rope was in good condition, and measured four inches in circumference. After a considerable delay Jumbo found himself a prisoner bound literally hand and foot, a position of affairs which apparently did not improve his temper. He now refused the biscuits and buns which were offered to him. Some shutters were no sooner screwed in than they were knocked on to the ground by the indignant elephant. A loud cheer from those assembled followed this exploit. It was then resolved to fasten him in at once by means of iron girders and wooden planks, which were ready at hand to be put through iron clamps front and back. The men had to climb to the roof of the box, which was being rocked with considerable violence by its occupant. In his desperation Jumbo dashed his head against an iron girder, thereby cutting his forehead, and chipping a small piece off one of his tusk stumps. The whole of the morning until one o'clock was occupied in getting Jumbo securely caged."

"The Last of Jumbo"

Once Jumbo was safely chained in his crate, the arduous journey to America began. According to *Lloyd's*, "Three hours more were occupied in clearing the way, and then seven horses were harnessed to the structure. - Jumbo thrust his trunk through the bars, and amused himself by trying to reach the shaft horses, but Scott, from his place upon the platform, grasped the active member and kept it out of mischief. Buns and oranges were again offered and readily accepted, and Scott seized the opportunity to administer a score or so of onions, which the elephant conveyed to his mouth, and with marvelous celerity returned his trunk at "the present." Henceforth, though the haulings and stoppages were frequent and tedious, Jumbo behaved himself remarkably well. At one o'clock on Thursday morning a team of 10 horses was attached to the van, and after a few fruitless efforts a start was made. The van ran briskly to the gateway, but it crashed into one of the posts and held fast, half in the road and half in the gardens. This caused some half-hour's delay, at the end of which time a clear start was made. Proceeding by way of Albany-street, Euston-road, King'a-cross, Gray's inn-road, Clerkoilwell prison, Uncommercial street, Lemau-street, and Nightingale-lane. No obstruction was met with on the route, and the only manifestation of Jumbo's disapproval of the proceedings was an occasional trumpet-like blast, which was heard above the clatter of the horses' feet. It may be incidentally remarked that if Scott left his position on the platform in front of the elephant's van for even a moment, Jumbo began to show signs of uneasiness, which, on his keeper's re-appearance, at once subsided."

Scott noted that Jumbo wasn't a terribly big fan of his modes of transportation: "I have considerable difficulty with Jumbo when travelling on the steam cars, for then Jumbo is like the dog in the manger. He can neither sleep himself, nor will he let me sleep. The shaking and jar of the train, the worrying noises, etc., keep him in a constant ferment of nervous excitement, and he gives me little chance for sleep. I no sooner get just nicely off into a dose than his trunk is groping into my little bed, feeling all round my body to find my face, to ascertain if I am there, so as to awake me to talk to him. Sometimes he is so fidgety during the night that neither of us get any sleep at all. Jumbo gets worried by this mode of travelling to such an extent that if I do not get up to talk to him when he calls me, as above described, he begins to lash his trunk against the sides of the car, and to save the car from being broken to pieces I have to get up and play with and talk to him."

Once the movers got the elephant through the streets of London to the pier, more difficult work commenced. According to the *Lloyd's* account, The docks were reached at about half-past five in the morning, the distance of about five miles having been accomplished in four hours, including stoppages. Stout hempen ropes were passed around the structure in which Jumbo was confined, and both the elephant and his temporary prison van—weighing between 10 and 11 tons—were hoisted into the air, and gradually lowered into the barge Clarence, which floated alongside the dock. Here he remained until the afternoon tide. The lady who has been in such constant attendance upon Jumbo in the Zoological Gardens was down at St. Katharine's docks, and before he started gave him nearly a couple of gallons of ale, of which he is very fond, and three half-quartern loaves. After this it is also somewhat sad to have to confess that he partook of some whisky that was offered to him with a relish that showed he was no true disciple of the school that Sir Wilfrid Lawson leads. Not only did he drink the whisky, but, like Oliver Twist, 'asked for more' in as plain language as an elephant is capable of doing. At a quarter to one o'clock the order was given to more, and the barge was hauled along the side of the dock. While all around seemed excited, Jumbo looked quite at home. He was slowly taken round the side of the dock till the barge reached the entrance, when the gates were opened, and the craft, with its strange freight, passing through, entered the Thames at 10 minutes past one. Some of the large steamers lying at rest at this part of the river readily made way for it, and it was soon made fast to a small river steamer, and quickly towed down the river. The voyage was pleasant, and occupied about three-quarters of an hour."

Just as he was beginning to come to terms with his situation, Jumbo was moved again. The article explained, "On reaching the spot opposite a large crane at the side of the dock, arrangements were made for taking Jumbo in his cage on land again. The elephant and box were lifted on shore by an immense crane, the box being lowered on two large blocks of timber, where it remained for the night. As many guesses had been hazarded as to how heavy the elephant was, the gross weight of the box and animal was taken by the automatic weighing machine attached to the derrick, and was proved to be 12 tons and a half, a figure which would show Jumbo, when in condition, to weigh over seven tons. Jumbo passed a "quiet night" in his box on the South quay, Millwall docks, and showed no signs of restlessness such as he exhibited during the early part of his transit. His keeper Scott was on duty all night, and this no doubt contributed to the composure of the animal. Shortly after noon on Friday, the Assyrian Monarch moved from her mooring at Messrs. Faton's warehouse to the south side of the Miliwall dock for the purpose of taking Jumbo on board. That long-suffering animal appeared to take things philosophically, and gazed quietly out of his box, which was stationed under the sheerleg's ready for shipment. He was surrounded by an admiring, but by no means complimentary crowd, the majority of whom were dock labourers, who spent their dinner-hour in gazing on the manacled brute. But among them was a very fair sprinkling of ladies and children, many of whom had brought with them presents, ' which, however, Jumbo refused to receive."

Finally, the time came for Jumbo to board the ship that would be trans-Atlantic home for a few weeks. The newspaper told readers, "At one o'clock Captain Harrison had his ship warped closely to the dock side; and the few privileged spectators who were admitted on the invitation of the owners came on board. They had hardly reached the fore-deck when the signal to commence hoisting was given. The powerful steam crane was at once set in motion, but it was almost immediately stopped working, as the flooring of No. 2 hatch was not complete. This flooring has been raised a couple of feet above the main deck, in order to make provision for drainage. While the caulkers were at work, the visitors amused themselves in watching all the arrangements which had been made for Jumbo's comfort on board. Captain Harrison has had considerable experience in carrying elephants, for in 1866, as an officer of the Daniel Webster, he brought four safely into port, although his ship encountered heavy weather, and was dismasted. In 1863 he also brought home an elephant from India. At 2.25 the second signal was given to commence hoisting, and the steam gear was set in motion. In the short space of 10 minutes Jumbo was slung over the port side of the vessel, and, amid the cheers of the several hundred spectators, safely landed in his berth. His two keepers, Scott and Newman, were with him during the whole of the operation. Although Jumbo once or twice protruded his trunk through the bars of his cage, and swayed to and fro, he was not unduly restive, and appeared to be quite resigned to his fate. In fact, he took matters very coolly, and gazed quietly at the many spectators who had come to take a last long look at the idol of the hour. A workman who had, however, the temerity to stay in the hold for a few moments, afraid the animal had not been safely deposited, got a gentle reminder of the brute's presence in the form of a push upwards, which resulted in the unfortunate man hurrying up the hatch-ladder in double-quick time, greatly to the amusement of the spectators."

With its precious cargo loaded, there was nothing to wait on, and the *Assyrian Monarch* left England's shores. The article concluded, "Jumbo had not been on board more than five minutes when the moorings were let go, and the vessel steamed across the dock to its berth at the company's wharf. ... Once out in the stream, everything worked well, and Jumbo, who occupies perhaps the most comfortable travelling berth in the ship, was unconscious of any peculiar motion. Gravesend was reached about eight o'clock, the arrival of the vessel being witnessed by nearly half the population of the town. Decked from bowsprit to mizen peak with flags of all nations, the Union Jack, and the Stars and Stripes floating out in the Springbreeze side by side, the arrival created quite a sensation. Large numbers of persona put off in boats in the hope of getting on board and obtaining a sight of Jumbo, but in this they were disappointed. Shortly after one the Baroness Baroness Burdett Coutts, Mr. Ashmead-Bartlett, Lord and Lady Tenterden, and several other visitors arrived on board the Assyrian Monarch, to wish Jumbo bon voyage. They all came laden with presents, which were handed to his charge by his keeper, Scott, and devoured with eagerness, and rapidity. At two o'clock the signal was given to clear decks, but, as usual, this operation too3c a long time, several officers of the Guards, who had hired a launch for the occasion, being the last, to leave. The vessel then steamed from the buoy, amid the cheers of the spectators, and proceeded slowly down the river. The food provided by Mr. Davis for the elephant up on his passage, which will be about 13 days, is two tons of hay, three sacks of oats, two of biscuits, and one of onions, a delicacy of which Jumbo is exceedingly fond."

Perhaps not surprisingly, this leg of the trip was uncomfortable for the famous passenger, as the *New York Times* pointed out: "Notwithstanding Mr. Barnum's assertion that elephants are never sick at sea, it was reported in the surgeon's books that Jumbo was decidedly "under the weather" during seven days of the trip. It was said that he hung his trunk on the bar in front of his box in a listless way and refused his usual rations during those days."

Fortunately, a break in the passage gave Jumbo a chance to better acclimate himself to his surroundings. The *Times* continued, "The room on the shelter and main decks which might have been occupied by 800 emigrants was cleared in consequence of placing Jumbo's box in the hatchway between these decks. The vessel 409 emigrant and 18 cabin passengers. On the first day out Jumbo was much excited and trumpeted a great deal. On the second day he subsided and began to show signs of illness. After seven days he had fully recovered, and was able to partake of bay, oats, bread, fruit, and onions with much relish. Mr. Scott and Mr. Newman watched him closely, and had two assistants. Jumbo was never alone. Mr. Newman said that a lady sent 18 dozen fine oysters for Jumbo and that he (Mr. Newman) and Mr. Scott enjoyed them."

Jumbo made the entire voyage in his crate, though only his feet remained chained while aboard ship. Meanwhile, Barnum busied himself with stirring up even more interest in his new project. He wrote stories about the elephant and placed them in waterproof bags that he then dropped into the ocean. As they washed up weeks later, people were delighted to learn small details about the elephant's voyage to his new home.

Assyrian Monarch in *The Pictorial World*, **1882**

Chapter 5: The Largest Living Mountain of Flesh to Travel the United States

"Jumbo, an African male elephant, the largest living mountain of flesh to travel the United States since the disappearance of the mammoth and mastodon, arrived in New York in March, 1882. His height was ten feet ten inches at the shoulder, and he weighed approximately 16,500 pounds. He was shipped in a heavily built crate that weighed probably nearly as much as he did. Low wheels of heavy iron were fastened to a truck under the crate and twenty-two horses hauled it from the docks to the old Madison Square Garden, where he was on exhibition for one month.

Then, with twenty-four other elephants, he made the trip to Brooklyn, crossing over the Brooklyn bridge. The following week he was loaded in an especially constructed car built for his accommodation at Jersey City. Because of his refusal to go into the car, chains were fastened around each foreleg and drawn through heavy rings that had been made fast to the floor of the car. In this way his front legs were drawn into the car, then two of the largest elephants were placed behind him with their heads to his rump and given an order to push. Jumbo did not like this and resisted by surging back as hard as possible. Finally he was conquered and safely chained. He kept the car rocking for hours and was greatly frightened when the train was moving." - William H. Blackburne

A depiction of Jumbo's arrival in New York

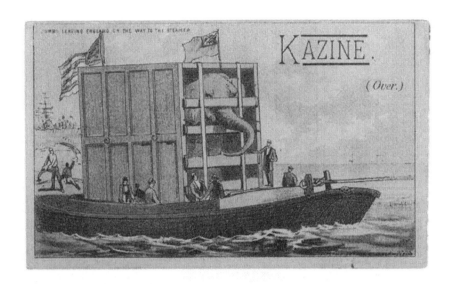

A card depicting Jumbo on a barge in New York

Jumbo joined thousands of other immigrants in arriving at New York Harbor just after midnight on April 9, 1882. As soon as word spread that the beloved elephant had at last made it to American shores, crowds gather to welcome him and to try to get a look at the beast. The *New York Times* described the scene: "Messrs. P. T. Barnum, James L. Hutchinson, James A. Bailey, George S. Bailey…and a few newspaper reporters shivered in the raw atmosphere of Castle Garden pier at an early hour yesterday morning, and stared at the steam-ship Assyrian Monarch, which was anchored in midstream. The famous elephant Jumbo was on board this vessel, and It was agreed by the party on the pier that the whole world was breathlessly awaiting intelligence of the beast's health and state of mind. Mr. Barnum was in an unusually happy mood, and assured the party that the event recalled the arrival of Jenny Lind in this country many years ago. Then he rattled off numerous anecdotes concerning the great singer. The small steamer Only Son hove in sight, and the enthusiasm of the party increased as the prospect of beholding Jumbo became more apparent. In a few moments the party was safely on board the Only Son, and Mr. Barnum began to explain that elephants are never sick at sea, and that therefore Jumbo would not be found under the care of a physician. Capt. John Harrison, of the Assyrian Monarch, welcomed his guests, and informed Mr. Barnum that Jumbo had behaved grandly through the voyage. Then the party descended a gangway to what was called the shelter deck. Here William Newman, sometimes called "Elephant Bill," was found. Mr. Newman had been sent to London in January for the purpose of accompanying Jumbo to this country. Like all elephant trainers he is excessively modest in the presence of human beings, and blushed like a schoolgirl when Mr.

Barnum congratulated him on his safe arrival."

Newman had good reason to be modest, for he was not the one who had made Jumbo's trip bearable for the poor animal. According to the article, even Barnum, never one to willingly share the spotlight, acknowledged this. "'Where's Scott?' shouted the veteran showman, and everybody took up the cry, "Where's Scott ?" the modest little man who owned this name quickly made his appearance. He has been with Jumbo since 1885, and this is his first visit to America."

What Scott thought of the condition in which his charge had been transported never made the papers, but they make the modern reader cringe with pity. The *Times* reported, "The party were led to the hatchway between the main and the upper decks, where Jumbo stood in a great iron bound box. The beast's trunk was, swung aloft on the outside, as though in expectation of buns or fruit, such as the children used to supply him in the Royal Zoological Gardens in London. The merest glance at the beast showed that he was of immense size, but upon closer inspection it was seen that he had extraordinarily long legs, and that his great height is due to their length. His countenance was as expressionless as the countenance of all elephants. His ears were of unusual size, and it was said that when they are spread like an eagle's wings they measure 15 feet from tip to tip. The tusks were not visible, having been lost years ago in a battle with an iron door Everybody, of course, asked the question, 'What is his height?' and Elephant Bill quietly replied, 'Eleven and a half' Some in the party thought that Jumbo was scarcely taller than the tallest of those in the herd at Madison Square Garden. Mr. Barnum came to the rescue of those who seemed disappointed in the elephant's height by saying that it should be understood that there is a considerable differences between the actual and the 'museum' height of elephants. Eleven and a half feet, he said, was the actual height of Jumbo. Then, everybody was happy, and looked with increased pride upon the beast. The box in which Jumbo was incased was said to be 12 ½ feet high, 13 feet long and 6 feet wide, and to all appearances he had abundance of room in which to swagger as all elephants swagger. The box and elephant weighed together 12 1/2 tons."

Not knowing what to give an arriving pachyderm, the people of New York feted their new celebrity with fancy foods and drink. The *Times* recorded, "A great many packages of food, bottles of champagne and beer were also sent by kind-hearted women and children for Jumbo's use, and the beast freely partook of the liquid refreshments. When Mr. Barnum heard this and remembered that he is an apostle of temperance, he said ' I am afraid Jumbo has been too liberally supplied with beer for many years ' Then he looked at Mr. Scott, Jumbo's keeper, and remarked, 'That animal's growth has been stunted by the use of beer.' Mr. Scott shook his head in a negative way, and as everybody laughed, First Officer Kidder said, ' Why, Jumbo is as fond of whisky as he is of beer.' ' Oh, no,' said Mr. Barnum sadly, 'don't say that' 'If you don't believe it, I'll prove it to you,' replied Mr. Kidder, and he hastily procured a bottle of whisky. Removing the cork from the bottle he poured the contents into the mouth of Jumbo s trunk. The elephant stood motionless and apparently in raptures until the last drop was emptied from the bottle. Then Jumbo curled an trunk up to his capacious mouth and poured the whisky into it.

Then he shook himself like a man who had been searching for his morning cocktail, and had at last been comforted by procuring it. 'I protest, I protest!' shouted Mr. Barnum, but it was too late."

He may have been unhappy with his elephant's lack of temperance, but Barnum was otherwise in his element, bantering with reporters and showing off for the crowd. "Then everybody asked questions, and were told marvelous stories about the enormous expense of transporting Jumbo from London to this port. Mr. Barnum said that the purchase of Jumbo and the expenses attending the lawsuits m London, his fare on the steam-ship, the cost of excluding so many emigrants from the vessel and countless other expenditures, would amount to fully $30,000. No duty would be paid on the elephant at this port, as Mr. Barnum had procured an order from the Secretary of the Treasury permitting him to land Jumbo without paying duty for him. 'I paid £2,000 for Jumbo for breeding purposes,' said Mr. Barnum, 'and would not in the first instance have paid, $3,000 for him for show purposes. If there had not been so much fuss made about him in London I would not have been so anxious to get him.' While Mr. Barnum and his party continued to gaze at Jumbo, small boats were conveying from the New York shores persons who had tickets of invitation to see Jumbo. Mr. D. O'Connor, the Passenger Agent of the Monarch Line of steam-ships, arrived with a large party, and later Mr. Edward Mott, the stalwart showman of Mr. Barnum's establishment, made his appearance. Then Superintendent Hartfield for the Society for the Prevention of Cruelty to Children, with an officer of that society, arrived and were shown to Jumbo's quarters. Everybody desired to know whether Jumbo was of a peaceful disposition, and Mr. Barnum assured them that he was 'perfectly Iamb-like,' adding that he was the idol of the children."

Interestingly enough, not everyone sang Jumbo's praises. The article noted, "One of the other showmen said that he doubted Jumbo's lamb-like disposition, and gave a bit of information which he had picked up from one of the crew. According to the seafaring man, Mr. Scott, Jumbo's Keeper, was afraid to enter the box during the voyage in order to clean it, and Mr. Newman, the American trainer, tried the plan adopted by elephant trainers in this country."

Always the showman, Barnum had carefully planned Jumbo's arrival, as the *Times* pointed out: "At about 3:30 o'clock the welcome intelligence was received that the Captain of the light had been captured. Then all hands were piped on deck. Steam was gotten up on the lighter, and the hatches over Jumbo's box were removed. By this time the neighboring sheds on the piers were black with men and boys, and its was said that fully 10,000 persons were standing around the Battery, eager for a look at Jumbo or the box containing him. The lighter was brought alongside the steamship and great chains were hauled to the deck of the latter vessel. ... By 4:30 o'clock much ado was made about putting the chains around his box, and the spectators judged from the way in which he swaggered that he was becoming unduly excited. When Mr. Scott's old familiar face appeared at the front of the box, however, Jumbo seemed assured that everything was all right. ... It was counted upon as almost certain that when the box was hoisted high above the deck of the vessel and was swung to one side so that it might be lowered to the deck of the lighter, the ropes or chains would break. While in this unhappy frame of mind the spectators were startled by a crash of wood. The signal had been given for the engineer of the lighter to 'hoist away,' and as the chains around the box were drawn tightly together the edges of the box were torn. 'Stop her,' was shouted by a thousand voices. Captain Harrison and Mr. Farnin stood on the roof of the box. ... The box was slowly lowered to the deck of the lighter without mishap and the crowds on the vessels and of the piers gave three hearty cheers for Jumbo. Mr. Scott, who had accompanied him in his aerial flight, stepped from the ledge of the box on which he had been standing, and many men warmly shook his hand."

By this time, Barnum had as much of a crowd as even he could dream of. According to the *Times*, "At 7 o'clock the lighter was towed toward the Battery pier, where nearly 2,000 persons were congregated. ... The passengers on the lighter examined the box and found scrawled with pencil on the outside expressions of endearment for Jumbo, evidently written by children in London. At the Battery pier the box was raised from the lighter. The truck with its four heavy and very small wheels was placed under it, and in the darkness and rain men set to work to get the truck in its proper place. The crowd became almost exasperated at the delay in getting this truck arranged. 'Why don't they take Jumbo from the box and permit him to walk up Broadway?' was heard on all sides. ...Mr. Bailey said he would not take the risk, fearing that Jumbo might attack the crowds. Sixteen horses arrived from the Madison-Square Garden. Eight of them were attached to the truck and an attempt was made to move the box, but a like attempt to move one of the piers of the East River bridge would bars been equally as successful. A long rope was attached to the forward part of the truck, and 400 or 600 men took hold and triad to assist the horses, but the wheels would not revolve. At 10 o'clock it was found that some other means must be adopted, and Mr. Bailey gave an order to one of his assistants to go to the Madison-Square Garden and procure 'some elephants.' While Gypsy and Chief, the proud father of the famous 'baby elephant,' were ambling down Broadway, the 16 horses, after numerous vain attempts, much consequent swearing among the drivers, and volumes of advice from the bystanders, suddenly, at just 11 o'clock, pulled the huge box and its contents from the rut into which it had sunk to the hard pavement. There rose a wild hurrah from the hundreds of spectators, and Jumbo trumpeted a response."

Those who braved the bad weather to watch the spectacle were not disappointed. The reporter from the *Times* insisted, "The strangest procession which ever passed up Broadway moved toward Madison-Square Garden In the pouring rain. First came the monster box, its eight horses, driven by Johnson, "the best driver In the world." Gypsy and Chief stalked solemnly after them on either side of their keeper. Behind them follow came the other eight horses, and a long, motley procession of men and women, boys and children brought up the rear. At Liberty Street the huge wagon stuck in a pile of earth thrown up from the excavations where the steam pipes are being laid and the two elephants in the rear placed their big heads against the back of the wagon and aided the horses to start it again. ... On arrival at the Madison Square Garden two of the teams of horses were taken off and tow elephants were put behind to push but when the box was brought near the door on the Fourth Avenue end, next to Twenty Seventh Street, it was found to be too tall to enter the doorway. By pulling and pushing it was then placed against the doorway, front forward and when The Times' reporter came away…it stood there on the sidewalk with Jumbo in it, gazing into the scene of his future triumphs."

Madison Square Garden as it looked in 1879

Jumbo and Scott in America in 1882

Chapter 6: I Had My Doubts

"I had a great feat to perform in New York City the second year after our arrival in America. … I was invited to take Jumbo for a processional walk over the great Brooklyn Bridge so as to test its strength. Of course ' the greatest showman of the earth ' — Mr. P. T. Barnum — had a business' object in view; but even he, with his vast and comprehensive mind, hardly realized the grandeur of the show he was about to give to the thousands and tens of thousands of the people of the United States…. Every available space on the tops of the towers and other high places of advantage, as well as on the banks of the river, was covered by thousands upon thousands of human beings, of all kinds and colors, and from all climes, gazing upon the greatest and most sublime works of man and God…. I had my doubts about the experiment of marching Jumbo over this great structure. I calculated that if I could coax him into keeping up regular marching order I might possibly get through the performance with safety, but then I also knew if he would commence any of his antics up aloft on that bridge, and begin to dance a hornpipe, so to speak, I expected he would shake the whole concern down into the river." - Scott

Advertising trade cards of Jumbo

Unfortunately, Jumbo's triumphant life in the United States would be short lived, but in the time the elephant spent in America, he more than earned his keep, entertaining more than 20,000 people on any given day by doing nothing more than being a gentle giant from a far off land. Later, he also gave rides, using the same howdah he had in London.

Though he never harmed a human being, Jumbo was not above taking his wrath out on his own home, occasionally knocking out bits of the Elephant House in which he lived when he was not traveling. Even Barnum could not complain about the expense of repairs, since Jumbo earned him about $1.5 million in the first year he was in America. Later estimates claim that more than 20 million people visited the elephant during his stay in the United States.

Of course, the truth was that Jumbo was rarely home long enough to cause trouble, as he was instead forced to spend most of his time on the road. Scott noted the extent of the travels, writing, "It was thought by the people of England that Jumbo could not be brought to see the American nation. It was held — and a good deal of pressure was brought to bear upon me, to the effect — that I should never be able to make the voyage across the Atlantic in safety with so monstrous an animal, and that the risk anyway was too great. It was also held by some that, as there were thousands of Americans coming to London every season, it was too risky a speculation or enterprise to pay, as the most of such visitors would have seen Jumbo in London. I am sometimes tickled a bit, when I think of the tens of thousands of miles Jumbo and I have travelled in the interior of this country since we made the perilous journey of three thousand miles by sea to the American shores; and I often wonder what the people of the old country will say to me when they hear of our travels out West, North, and South, or what they will say to me when we get back to our own shores."

In 1884, Jumbo performed perhaps his most famous act in America by being one of a small herd of elephants to test out the newly completed Brooklyn Bridge. As the giant animals trudged across the span, the bridge creaked but remained solid, inviting the human population to also make its way safely to the other side. The *New York Times* reported, "England's pet, old Jumbo, his loyal sacredness, the white elephant, and the mighty name of Barnum added new luster to the bridge last night. To people who looked up from the river at the big arch of electric lights it seemed as if Noah's Ark were emptying itself over on Long Island. At 9:30 o'clock 21 elephants, 7 camels, and 10 dromedaries issued from the ferry at the foot of Courtlandt-Street…. The other elephants shuffled along, raising their trunks and snorting as every train went by. Old Jumbo brought up the rear."

Late 19th century illustration depicting the Brooklyn Bridge

However, by the time Jumbo lumbered across that bridge, his health was already beginning to fail. Too many sweets and not enough good, simple hay had caused his teeth to decay, and it was becoming increasingly difficult for him to eat. Barnum was obviously more showman than animal lover, and he insisted that his investment continue earning its keep, even while he made private plans to have the elephant put down and taxidermied when the time came.

As it turned out, Jumbo was relieved of his suffering sooner than anyone anticipated. He met his end on September 15, 1885, in a rail yard in St. Thomas, Ontario, while touring Canada. Following their last performance of the evening, Jumbo and the other elephants were led through the rail yard to their own cars. The circus train extended along a long track on their right, while their left side was blocked by an embankment. Suddenly, a previously unscheduled train bore down on the group, approaching from the east. As soon as the engineer saw the animals, he tried to stop, and most of those in line escaped injury, but poor Jumbo was at the end of the line and could only try to outrun the coming disaster.

Scott was with the elephant, running alongside the track and urging him on, but the giant beast was not fast enough. The train eventually struck the massive elephant, causing his body to become wedged under a flatcar. The *Williamsport Warren Republican* reported, P. T. Barnum's $10,000 pet elephant was killed half a mile east of here on the Grand Trunk Air-Line track Tuesday evening. While being led along the track to his car he was run down by a freight train and so badly injured that he died in thirty minutes. The trick elephant Tom Thumb, had his leg broken. ... Barnum received the news of the death of Jumbo while at breakfast yesterday morning in the Murray Hill Hotel Mr. Barnum was very much affected, and said that Jumbo's death ended the project of taking the show to Europe next year, as had been intended."

Jumbo was only 24 years old, early middle age for an elephant, yet Barnum managed to figure out a way to try to profit off this misfortune. In the wake of the elephant's death, Barnum released a dramatic tale to the press about how Jumbo had died trying to save the smaller elephant, Tom Thumb, from being hit, but the truth was not nearly as heroic. The train engine hit and injured the younger elephant first, which was enough to derail the train, and Jumbo was hit directly by the derailed train and killed.

Jumbo after being hit by the train

A newspaper illustration of Jumbo saving the younger elephant

Barnum in 1885

After his death, Barnum continued to exhibit portions of Jumbo's body before ultimately donating the skeleton to the American Museum of Natural History in New York. He also had the elephant's skin taxidermied and displayed wherever the circus traveled over the next two years. In fact, over the ensuing years, Barnum continued trying to make the best of the situation, at least for himself. As he put it:

> "Since Jumbo was the most wonderful elephant that ever lived, I may as well give you all that is known about him. He was twenty-three years old when he died, and as elephants cease growing only when they attain the age of thirty, we began to have great fears as to how we should get him through the numerous railroad tunnels of the country. He was within five or six inches of the height of an ordinary railroad tunnel when he died. ... You have learned of his affecting death by a railway accident, and perhaps have seen his mounted skeleton, now with my show. I had him mounted by Professor Henry A. Ward, of Rochester, New York, who made careful measurements, which he reported to

me, as follows, which I believe are now published for the first time:

Circumference (6 inches back of the eye), 10 feet 4 inches.

Largest diameter of the ear, 5 feet 5 inches. (Jumbo was an African elephant.)

Circumference of tusk at the base, 1 foot 6 inches.

Circumference of trunk at base, 3 feet 5 inches.

Length of trunk from base of tusk, 5 feet 1 1 inches.

Body circumference, just back of shoulders, 16 feet 4 inches.

Body circumference at middle,- 18 feet.

Body circumference at point in front of hind legs, 17 feet. Length of tail, 4 feet 6 inches.

Fore legs: circumference of foot, 5 feet 3 inches.

Circumference of leg (3 feet above sole of foot), 3 feet 10 inches.

Hind legs : circumference of foot, 4 feet.

Circumference of leg (2 feet above sole of foot), 3 feet.

Circumference of leg (4 feet above sole of foot), 4 feet 8 inches.

Height, measuring from sole of foot to a point between shoulder-blades, about 12 feet.

Entire length of animal, 14 feet.

The heart weighed 46 pounds.

When alive Jumbo weighed 7 tons, and the weight of the mounted skeleton is about 3 tons."

The remains of Jumbo on display at Tufts University

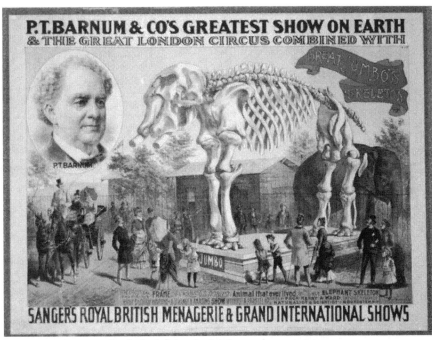

Jumbo's skeleton depicted on a circus poster

It's clear by the steps he took that Barnum insisted the show must go on, and of course it did, with acrobats performing daring acts and the ever popular General Tom Thumb. Following Jumbo's death, he and Bailey parted company, but the two reunited in 1888 with a new project, "Barnum & Bailey Greatest Show On Earth," later renamed the "Barnum & Bailey Circus." This venture was bigger than ever, and in addition to touring America, this circus toured the world. Barnum was determined, as he said, to "impress on the public that we are prepared to keep the show at the top of the heap for generations to come…" He certainly succeeded, as he and his circus became even more popular than ever.

Barnum was not sure how he or the circus would be received in London following the drama of taking Jumbo the elephant to the U.S. However, he had wanted to take his circus to Europe for a decade, and now that he was 79, it seemed that if he was going to do it, he should not wait much longer.

Apparently, all was forgiven by the Londoners, as the 100 day tour surpassed the hopes of Barnum and Bailey. The circus was not new to England, but a circus of this magnitude certainly had never been seen before on that side of the Atlantic. The flattering reviews lauded Barnum's talents as a showman and his willingness to stage the grandest spectacles ever seen. Barnum himself was in high demand, commanding audiences with the Prince and Princess of Wales, Prime Minister William Ewart Gladstone, the king of Greece, and any number of members of British high society and aristocracy. Even Queen Victoria did not miss the show.

After Barnum's death, his grandson continued to run the circus, but by 1907, he was tired of being in business and was ready to retire, so he sold the business to the country's other famous ringmasters: the Ringling Brothers. Although P.T. Barnum had never done business with the Ringling Brothers, his name is still intimately associated with the Ringling Brothers and the joint venture, and the Ringling Brothers were so aware of the popularity of Barnum's name that they kept it in the title of the circus despite the fact that Barnum had been dead for over 15 years when they bought out his nephew.

The Ringling Bros. and Barnum & Bailey Circus is still in operation today and very popular, but the circus may have been best immortalized in the 1952 film *The Greatest Show on Earth!*. The movie, which won the Best Picture, was a drama revolving around a few characters within the Ringling Bros. and Barnum & Bailey Circus, but in many ways, the circus itself was the star, as the review in *Variety* magazine noted when it said the film "effectively serve[s] the purpose of a framework for all the atmosphere and excitement of the circus on both sides of the big canvas." Shot in Technicolor, the film's visuals impressed audiences and critics alike, and critic Bosley Crowther captured what watching the film was like at the time: "Sprawling across a mammoth canvas, crammed with the real-life acts and thrills, as well as the vast backstage minutiae, that make the circus the glamorous thing it is and glittering in marvelous Technicolor—truly marvelous color, we repeat—this huge motion picture of the big-top is the dandiest ever put upon the screen."

A review in *Time* magazine may have summed it up best when it called the film a "mammoth merger of two masters of malarkey for the masses: P. T. Barnum and Cecil B. de Mille…[that] fills the screen with pageants and parades [and] finds a spot for 60-odd circus acts". Barnum himself noted that the "noblest art is that of making others happy", and while his methods were shady enough that he has come to be considered the epitome of a huckster, thanks to the presentation of acts like Jumbo, Barnum at least could claim he spent his life doing just that.

Online Resources

Other 19th century American history titles by Charles River Editors & Sean McLachlan

Other titles about Jumbo on Amazon

Bibliography

Barnum, Phineas Taylor (1889), The Wild Beasts, Birds and Reptiles of the World: The Story of Their Capture, R. S. Peale & Company

Bondeson, Jan (1999), The Feejeee Mermaid and Other Eassays in Natural and Unnatural History, Cornell University Press, ISBN 0-8014-3609-5

Chambers, Paul (2008), Jumbo: This Being the True Story of the Greatest Elephant in the World, Steerforth Press

Culhane, John (1990), The American Circus: An Illustrated History, Henry Holt and Company, Inc., ISBN 0-8050-0424-6

Haley, James L. (August 1973), "The Colossus Of His Kind: Jumbo", American Heritage 24 (5)

Harding, Les (2000), Elephant Story: Jumbo and P. T. Barnum Under the Big Top, McFarland, ISBN 978-0-7864-0632-6

Kotar, S. L.; Gessler, J. E. (2011), The Rise of the American Circus, 1716–1899, Jefferson, NC: McFarland, ISBN 978-0-7864-6159-2

MacDonald, Cheryl (2009), Celebrated Pets: Endearing Tales of Companionship and Loyalty, Heritage House Publishing Co., ISBN 978-1-894974-81-3

New York Times. 16 September 1885. Great Jumbo Killed ...

Ogden, Tom (1993), Two Hundred Years of the American Circus: From Abba-Daba to the Zoppe-Zavatta Troupe, Facts On File, Inc., ISBN 0-8160-2611-4

Preston, Douglas J. (1986), Dinosaurs in the Attic: An Excursion Into the American Museum of Natural History, Macmillan, ISBN 0-312-21098-1

Saxon, A. H. (1989), P. T. Barnum: The Legend and the Man, Columbia University Press, ISBN 0-231-05686-9

Wilson, Susan (2002), "An Elephant's Tale", Tufts Magazine, Spring

Scott, Matthew (1885). The autobiography of Matthew Scott and his biography of P.T. Barnum's great elephant Jumbo. ISBN 978-1-480-10798-4.